I0169528

"You are my sun, my moon, and all of my stars."

—E.E. Cummings

To my dear daughters,
Melissa, Shayna, and Lauren:
I treasure your love, friendship,
wisdom, and strength.
Love you forever and beyond.

Contents

Disclaimer: The advice in this book is not a substitute for medical or psychiatric advice. Rather, you can use it as an adjunct to professional medical assistance in helping you heal your mind, body, and spirit.

Acknowledgments

I want to thank Lawrence Knorr, owner and publisher of Sunbury Press, for his valuable help, enthusiasm, and kindness. Thanks also to Crystal Devine, Production Manager at Sunbury Press, for her excellent assistance and willingness to listen and respond during the editing process.

Introduction:
Note to the Reader

We know unequivocally that harnessing the power of the mind by meditating and saying affirmations can help heal your mind, body, and spirit. This book targets readers who would like to get in touch with their spiritual selves to access their innate healing powers. If you are presently on an advanced path and are already deeply immersed in spirituality, you can also benefit from using these spiritual tools. It's important to keep in mind that all of the meditations, manifestations, and affirmations in this book relate to the principles of Mindfulness that emphasize being present in the moment, rather than living in the past or worrying about the future.

Regardless of where you are on your spiritual journey, you will find it comforting and relaxing to say the words, visualize the colors, and use the other senses, such as taste, touch, and smell, contained in the meditations. The "Manifest Now" sections of the book reinforce the power of each meditation by giving you words and gestures that amplify the power of the meditation. Finally, the affirmations will boost your efforts to soothe your mind, body, and spirit. I encourage you to supplement these affirmations with ones you write yourself and include simple instructions on how to do this.

Consider This

Before each meditation, you'll find a section called "Consider This" that invites you to think more deeply about how the topics listed in the table of contents relate to your unique situation. This section can act as a springboard to help you consider additional aspects of the topics that reflect your concerns and how you can best help yourself remedy them.

Here are a few things you'll want to do to help make your experience using this book more effective and rewarding: Before doing each meditation, relax your mind completely. Take at least two slow deep breaths or as many as you need to help you relax. Breathe in through your nose and out through your mouth. Before beginning each meditation, picture a pleasant scene that brings you peace and tranquility, such as a soft, sandy beach with a cool blue/green surf, or any experience that translates as the ultimate relaxation scene for you. Position yourself in the middle of this scene, and luxuriate in its peacefulness.

When you take a few minutes to bring yourself to this blissful state, you'll find yourself more receptive to the suggestions that follow. You may open or close your eyes, depending on whether you are reading or listening to your own recorded voice. Do whatever makes you feel comfortable.

How to Use the Meditations

Read the words of the meditation silently or aloud, whichever method works best for you. You can use one or more meditations each day. If you'd prefer, you can concentrate on doing one a couple of times a day. They're short, so you can easily fit them into your schedule. Try to practice the meditation at the same time every day until you see a positive change in the issue(s) you're striving to improve.

You'll find a lot of different ideas in the literature about using color to meditate. Many practitioners advise using specific chakra colors to address certain concerns. Some writers who use color therapy advocate meditating with one color, while others advise using another. While some of the meditations in this book go along with chakra colors and those advised by color therapists, at times, I recommend other colors I intuitively believe would complement the meditation.

If you feel strongly about using a certain color not advocated by chakra or color experts (or this book) for an issue that concerns you, try it to see how it works for you. I've found that people often know intuitively which colors work best for them.

If you find it challenging to visualize the colors mentioned, find the color on the web or look for one like it in a crayon box. If you'd prefer, gather some color chips from a paint shop to help you visualize the colors.

You don't need to go by the exact names on the colors of the crayons or paint chips. Think of how you would most clearly imagine how the color looks, and choose the one that looks the most similar to how you see it when you picture it. Try looking at the color until you can close your eyes and visualize it mentally. Then, as you do the meditation, the color will imprint itself on your mind.

After you complete the meditation, gradually open your eyes. Gently shake out your arms and hands and move your feet around. Sit for a few moments, and enjoy the afterglow until you feel like resuming activity.

Manifest Now
The "Manifest Now" section that follows each meditation reinforces the power of the meditation. It's beneficial to read and apply this section immediately after you emerge from the relaxation state of each meditation. When you say the words in the "Manifest Now" section, infuse them with deep expression and meaning. Make your body language strong and powerful, and, in your own way, make it match the words you say. Doing this will heighten the strength of your meditation and will make it more likely that what you're asking for will materialize.

How to Use the Affirmations

Following each "Manifest Now" Section, you'll find affirmations to help you further reinforce the power of the meditation. You may want to say the affirmations you're most drawn to a few times a day, like a mantra, to reinforce what you want to happen.

Say each affirmation slowly and with expression. Place a star (if you want, you can use those gold stars that teachers give kids for rewards) or a checkmark next to the affirmations that resonate most with you. Say the affirmations every day until you get the results you want. After that, use the affirmations whenever you feel the need to strengthen your mind, body, and spirit.

I encourage you to supplement the affirmations in this book with ones you create yourself. You can use the affirmations in this book to generate ideas, personalizing them with your own unique touches. Keep a special notebook where you write your own affirmations for the topics that most pertain to you. Try writing one or two of your own affirmations to add to the ones in this book.

Here are some suggestions for writing affirmations: Always use the present tense, not the future. You want whatever you're asking for to happen now. Be creative. Write your affirmations to read the way you talk. Use slang if you want, and let your own pet words and phrases personalize your affirmations, and tailor them to your personality. Choose words that move and inspire you. If you're a serious person, be serious;

if you're funny, make it light. In other words, write the way you talk to help you feel at ease when you say the affirmations you've created.

All of the meditations and manifestations in this book ask you to be in the moment, to be mindful of what you're saying and what you're requesting. Accordingly, the affirmations are about asking for good things to happen right now rather than in some far-off future. Ground yourself in the present moment, for that is what we have, not the past or the future, but the living, breathing now.

Enjoy your journey!

Note: To maintain inclusiveness in language, I vary the use of *he* and *she*.

1

Make Wise Decisions

Consider This

Making decisions isn't easy, especially if they're life-altering ones such as changing jobs, moving, or deciding whether to continue a relationship. What kinds of decisions give you trouble: small ones, like what to wear to work, or major ones, like whether to leave your job and find a new one? Making decisions can take up a lot of your time and cause you to question your choices.

When you think about it, your first instinct about making the right decision often serves you best. The more you consider all the pros and cons of one decision versus another and the longer you mull over it, the harder it becomes to make up your mind. In the long run, it helps to make your decision using your own best instincts. Trust the answer that comes to you now, the answer that feels like the best fit. You already know the right answer. All you have to do is act on it.

What decisions do you need to make? Stop for a moment and say the decision in your mind in question form: For example: Is it best for me to proceed this way or another way? List your options in writing. Now speak your question aloud, and the answer will come, if not now, in due time.

Meditation for Making Wise Decisions

Find a relaxing spot and settle comfortably into it. Now picture the color yellow as it appears in a fragrant yellow rose. See a whirling, swirling splash of yellow sending waves of clarity through your mind. You are starting to see your answer now.

When you picture yellow, your decision is clear, like the shimmering brightness of the color yellow. The dazzling yellow fortifies your body with strength and determination, so you are making your decision and standing by it. Now picture a perfect yellow rose. Touch its soft yellow petals, smooth as yellow velvet. Breathe in the fragrance of the yellow rose to the count of three. Exhale the yellow slowly, and feel your confidence building as you make your decision. Breathe the yellow in and out, in and out.

Manifest Now!

You are beginning to make your decision effortlessly. The answer is coming to you now. The answer may come to you loudly and clearly, or it will come to you in a small, whispered voice, one that you've heard before and know well. You know with certainty it's the right answer because it's the one you lean toward, the one that makes you feel most at ease and most comfortable. It's the best decision possible for you at this time. You don't have to think for a long time about your choices to make a decision that will work for you. It was there all along, waiting for you to embrace it, to say, "This is what I need to do now." Your decision is true, bright, and clear as the color yellow. Picture the clarity of the yellow rose. Picture holding the rose and breathing in its powerful scent.

With deep conviction, say the following words aloud: "What I decide is right for me. I am the only one who can decide, and the answer is clear to me. No one can decide for me better than I can. My decision fits me perfectly and leads me on the right path. I make my decision with faith and confidence. All is well."

Affirmations to Help You Make Wise Decisions

- I have the ability to know what is best for me in everything I do.
- I know how to make the best decisions for myself.
- When I look at my choices, the best one stands out above all others.
- I use both my common sense and my intuition to make a great decision.
- I have confidence that my decision serves me well.
- I look forward to seeing the good things that happen because of my decision.
- I am making the best decision possible for me at this time.

2

Boost Creativity

Consider This

One thing I'm sure you know is that creativity comes naturally. You can never force it, but it can be yours for the asking. For those times when you need inspiration, it often helps to surround yourself with activities you love to beckon your creative impulses. Listen to music, view art, write from your heart, and read poetry. Whatever moves you is always the best catalyst for inspiration. Then, when the muse descends, as she surely will, sing, dance, paint, write, or go where your creative drive leads you.

If your urge to be creative doesn't kick in when you want it to, don't worry. It will appear another time. Ask what's stopping you, what's blocking you. You can get past the excuses, procrastination, and dry periods. Start engaging in your creative task and see where it leads you. Often when you take the first step and gather your paints, sit down at your writing desk, or start playing music, your inspiration will be ready and waiting for you to take the next step.

Activate your creative powers. Let them flow freely from your soul, for that is where they always begin.

Meditation for Boosting Creativity

Name the creative endeavor you plan to pursue. Say exactly what you want your creative powers to bring you. Say it as if you are already doing it now. For example, "I am writing a book and publishing it; I am starting a business and succeeding at it; or, I am using watercolors to paint beautiful pictures for my own pleasure and satisfaction."

See yourself fully engaged in your creative act with all the props connected with it: paints, pens, paper, computer, a musical instrument, or whatever you need to help you realize your goal. Allow the color indigo, a deep sky blue, to flow into your brain. Think of the color indigo, a deep night-sky blue. All you can see is the sky with a sliver of the white moon peeking through. Breathe deep indigo blue in and out, in and out slowly until it suffuses your brain with creative energy to carry out your project to perfection.

Manifest Now!

Visualize the finished product born of your creative mind. See the book, the new business, or the work of art. Whatever it is, see it in your mind's eye. It is your unique creation. Touch the product you've created. Feel the fullness of the book, the effectiveness of the business plan, or the texture of the painting. Whatever you want to create, use your senses to make it real in your mind. Proclaim the beauty and timelessness of the creation that only you could make. Picture the indigo blue sky, its vastness and majesty, giving you power to create.

Say these words aloud with strength and conviction: "I create my best work now. I am fully inspired and engaged in my creativity. My creative powers drive and inspire me to make something unique, something beautiful. I am a partner in the creative process, a channel for the universal creative mind. All is well. It is done."

Affirmations to Help You Boost Creativity

- I use my creative powers to enhance my life to the fullest.
- Letting my creativity flow is easy and effortless.
- I am doing what I've always wanted to do.
- My creative powers kick in whenever I ask.
- Other people and I delight in what I create.
- Creative and unique ideas are coming to me now.
- I am always in the mood to use my creative talents.

3

Generate Prosperity

Consider This

Do you need prosperity to come into your life now? Sometimes you go through periods where money is scarce or not flowing as much as you'd like. You work many hours, and it seems there's nothing to show for it, or you can't figure out a way to get your business off the ground to realize a substantial profit. However, it doesn't have to be that way. You have the innate power to generate prosperity. Ask yourself what you can do to create the prosperity you need to live a comfortable life.

Do you feel stuck in old patterns that may be standing in the way of helping you reach your financial goals? Think about ways you can break the pattern and help yourself out of the situation you're currently experiencing. Believe that you will enjoy prosperity, that enough money will come your way. Believe it in your heart and your gut.

What is standing in the way of your prosperity? You alone know the reasons. Figure out what they are and take steps to find the prosperity you deserve. You are fully worthy of an abundant way of life that includes both spiritual and material prosperity. Think of the blessings you already have, and give thanks. Think of the people you love, your greatest spiritual resources, and give thanks.

Have faith that you will find a job commensurate with your talents and abilities, one that you love going to every day. Believe that your work will prosper in new and wondrous ways. You are finding a way to generate prosperity. With a positive outlook and creative thinking, you're on your way. The only way you can go is up.

Meditation for Generating Prosperity

You are finding ways to produce prosperity in your life so you may live the way you want to, without worry or fear. Funds are coming to you because of your ingenuity and resourceful thinking. You are thinking in ways you never did before about how to generate the exact amount of income you need.

Make yourself comfortable, and bring the color green into your mind. Envision it as a sign of hope to help you find the prosperity you need. Think of lush evergreen foliage in a mystical forest. Slowly breathe in and slowly exhale the deep, dark green of the evergreen trees in the forest until you feel it's a part of you and the abundance you seek. Breathe the deep green in and out, in and out.

Manifest Now!

Think of prosperity coming to you as you breathe in the color of evergreen, and know that you are using your creativity to think of ways to grant yourself the exact level of prosperity you need. Give thanks also for everything spiritual and material that you have. If you believe you need more, ask, and it will come your way. All you have to do is ask and believe it will happen for you.

Say these words aloud and believe they are happening now: "I am thinking of new ways to bring prosperity into my life. I am open to new ideas and paths I have not yet considered. Prosperity and abundance come my way because I am open to them and fully deserve them. I am a worthy person who asks and receives. It is done."

Affirmations to Help You Generate Prosperity

- Each day I find more ways to attract prosperity.
- I have the intelligence and resourcefulness I need to gain prosperity.
- I view prosperity as a positive, uplifting force in my life.
- I have the creativity and ingenuity to generate the funds I need.

- The money I need comes easily and effortlessly.
- I find great enjoyment in gaining the funds I need.
- I appreciate the prosperity I gain and share it with others.

4

Declutter Your Mind

Consider This

You already know the importance of taking the time to clear the clutter from your house. Some people become uncomfortable with small amounts of clutter, while others wait until they're snowed under by papers, clothes, and other things they've accumulated over the years. Whatever method you prefer for dealing with all the things you've saved but no longer need, you know that once you purge your home of excess baggage, you'll feel freer to appreciate the things you have.

Think about how decluttering your mind can bring about similar results to your sense of being able to live more freely, unencumbered by intrusive thoughts and worries about what may happen tomorrow that usually never materialize. Be curious and ask yourself what types of thoughts stand in the way of your making wise decisions, boosting creativity, generating prosperity, and living each day to the fullest.

We all accumulate our own unique type of mind-clutter. For many people, mind-clutter involves needless worry and recurring thoughts about their family's welfare or their own health concerns. If you find yourself constantly preoccupied with worrying about issues, such as whether the college your child prefers will offer acceptance or whether you're going to get the new job you've applied for, stop for a minute. Remind yourself that unnecessary worry will probably not change the outcome. Catch yourself in the act of cluttering your mind with thoughts that won't help and may sap the energy you need to help you reach your goals.

Whenever intrusive thoughts dominate your brain, or you fall captive to worries you can't do anything about, be curious and ask yourself how these thoughts will affect the outcome. Use self-talk to help you declutter your mind so you can think clearly and develop a plan to use your brain to find helpful solutions to any problems and worries you encounter.

Meditation to Help Declutter Your Mind

You are making a strong effort to declutter your mind so you can devote more mental energy to focus on the things that matter most to you. When you declutter your mind, you can enjoy the things that interest and intrigue you and make better decisions,

Sit comfortably and call upon the clear color of pure water flowing from a spring in a peaceful grotto. Slowly breathe in and exhale the pure clarity of spring water. Gather the precious liquid in a tin cup and relish the cool, fresh taste of water free of additives and contaminants. Breathe the clear color of fresh, clean water in and out, in and out.

Manifest Now!

Think of how free you will feel when you make an effort to minimize your mind clutter. Ask yourself what types of thoughts keep you from living a happy life, and then make a conscious effort to release them from your mind. Drink in the clarity of the crystal-clear spring water and banish worrisome thoughts.

Lift your eyes to the sky. Say these words, and believe in the new sense of freedom you realize when you declutter your mind: "I embrace only thoughts that serve me well and release those that intrude upon my peace of mind and clear thinking. My thoughts serve me well by helping me gain happiness, good health, and prosperity. And so, it is."

Affirmations to Help You Declutter Your Mind

- I live more freely when I declutter my mind of worries.
- I take the time to act curious about my thoughts.
- I know that worrying will not change the outcome.

- I catch myself when I clutter my mind with unimportant thoughts.
- I use self-talk to rid my mind of intrusive thoughts.
- I release all the clutter from my mind. I am free and at peace.
- I declutter my mind by releasing worries and useless thoughts.

5

Take a Break from News and Social Media

Consider This

You know the importance of keeping informed about world affairs and the news in your locality. However, news over-saturation can trigger stress and quickly transform your mood from cheerful to gloomy. Often, when you hear negative news stories repeated, you begin to feel tense and irritable. You may also find yourself quick to lash out at family and friends who share different political views or opinions about the current state of affairs.

To see how a constant barrage of negative news affects you, try limiting your intake by watching the news only once a day for a short period. Choose your time and stand by it. See how you feel after a week or two of modifying your daily dose of news. After you set a time limit on watching the news, ask a family member to tell you if she's noticed a difference in your mood or interactions with others. More important, monitor your feelings and reactions after you cut back on the news.

Taking a long or short break from social media also affords you a chance to be alone with your thoughts and to do more things you've put off. Hearing about people's problems on social networking sites can take its toll on your emotions, especially if you're empathetic. Worse, social media venues can sometimes set friend against friend and stir up controversy and animosity. Try limiting your time on social media to see if it helps you become more peaceful and productive.

Meditation for Taking a Break from News and Social Media

The noise and subliminal effects from news sound bites can bore into your subconscious mind and exhaust you. Watching the news or logging on to social media can offer an escape from the daily grind. However, if you overindulge in these pastimes, you may not participate in activities that bring you deeper and more lasting satisfaction, such as engaging in meaningful interactions with family and friends. When you take a break from the news or your favorite social media outlet, immediately notice how relaxed you feel.

Think of the color deep blue topaz when you ponder the rewards of taking a break from social media. The blue sparkles and imparts lasting energy to your mind and spirit, unlike the tiredness you may experience when you watch the news or access social media. Picture wearing a blue topaz ring set in silver. Focus on the deep blue stone that gleams and glimmers on your finger. Breathe the deep blueness in and out, in and out. Picture yourself rejuvenated, ready to enjoy the time you've gained by limiting your news and social media exposure.

Manifest Now!

Limit your news and social media intake to bring more freedom and relaxation to your life. Bask in the energizing light of deep blue topaz to feel the energy it transmits.

Sit comfortably. Place hands, palms up, on your knees, and say this: "I enjoy my time away from the news and social media. I substitute activities that enhance my connection with myself and others. I free myself to spend more time on the things I love, like enjoying my own company and nourishing my creativity. I am at peace."

Affirmations to Help You Take a Break

- I take time to observe the effects I feel from overusing news or social media.
- When I take a break from the news or social media, I feel more alive.
- When I minimize my exposure to news outlets or media networks, I find more time to enjoy life.

- After I take a break from the news or social media, I observe a positive change.
- I gain time to do things I love when I limit my news and social media exposure.
- I gain energy when I take a break from the daily news and social media.
- Limiting news and social media grants me more time with friends and family.

6

Follow Your Passion

Consider This

Many people don't attempt to follow their passion in life because they think it's impossible to attain. But if you don't try, how will you know if you can realize your heart's desire? What is it you want to do right now? Do you want to try a new job or work in a different capacity in your present job? Do you want to learn a new skill or take up a hobby you've never tried before? Do you want to travel to a place you've never seen? If there's something you've always thought of trying but never got around to, don't let anything stop you. Start following your passion today.

How will you discover your passion if you're not sure what it is? Think about the subjects you read about in books and on the internet. Think about the subjects you never tire of discussing with your friends. Your passion is what motivates you and propels you onward. It creates energy and excitement in your life. Now it's time to go after it and embrace it.

Meditation for Following Your Passion

Think about what you want to do above everything else, and snap a mental picture of doing it now. You are doing what you've always wanted to do. You see yourself in that picture. You see the sights and hear the sounds of participating in your passion. You are living everything in the picture and know it is real. You and your heart's desire are one. Blow the picture up, and post it on the wall of your mind. You are in the picture, and it is happening for you now.

Think of the color ruby red. Pick a ruby red rose, so fragrant you want to inhale it. Lift it to your nose and breathe, breathe, breathe it in. Keep breathing it in and out, in and out, until the intoxicating rose scent saturates the air around you. Think of your passion, and breathe in the red rose and your passion. They are one. You are finding your passion now. It is as fragrant and palpable as the perfect red rose.

Manifest Now!

You are fully engaged in your passion. It brings you joy and contentment like nothing you have ever felt before. Your passion transports you to that blissful state where time falls away, and eternity begins. Imagine holding a red rose in your hand. Smell the powerful scent, the scent of passion.

Say these words aloud with feeling, letting your voice rise and fall in all the right places to stress their meaning: "I am following my passion in life now. It is the path I need to take to realize complete happiness. The passion I crave is something I have always wanted. Until now, I have not acted on it, but today I will begin. My passion is what drives and consumes me. It is both a dream and a reality that I am discovering and participating in my passion. And so it is."

Affirmations to Help You Follow Your Passion

- Following my passion is a vital part of my life.
- I choose to do something each day to make my passion a reality.
- I am motivated and inspired to enjoy what I most want to do in life.
- I am finding my passion and loving my adventure.
- I choose to make my passion a major part of my life.
- When I am fully engaged in my passion, I feel a timeless bliss.
- My passion drives my life and completes me.

7

Live Each Day to
the Fullest

Consider This

It helps to wake up with a plan. Ask yourself how you
intend to spend each day to its best advantage. All you
really have is this day, this moment. Making the best
of it can help you reach your goals and live consciously
and authentically.

Who are the people in your life that matter most?
Let them know each day with words and actions how
important they are to you. Take the time to tell them
you love them, or give them a hug or kiss to show them
tangibly how much they mean to you. Little gestures,
like giving those you love a compliment or doing a
small favor, never go unnoticed and make love thrive.

What steps can you take each day to help you reach
the goals most important to you? They don't have to

be giant steps, but you'll move closer to reaching your goals if you take one action each day to point yourself in the right direction. If you want to look for a new job because you don't enjoy your present one, draw up a plan of action and start the process. If you want to travel to a place you've never seen, gather brochures, and make a decision. If you've always wanted to write, draw, paint, or take up a new hobby, start today. You know that many people put off things they value doing in hopes of doing them some day in the distant future. You've also seen that for many, that day never comes.

Each day ask yourself what you can do to move closer to your goals, make a plan, and start doing it. Now is the time to begin to live each day to the fullest.

Meditation for Living Each Day to the Fullest

Promise yourself today that you will start living life to the fullest. When you wake up each day, set specific goals that take you where you want to be in your relationships, in your job, and in the activities that bring joy to your spirit. Each day, bring yourself one step closer to the life you want to live, the best life possible for you.

Imagine the silky brown shell and the moist, sweet center of a chocolate-covered cherry. Picture eating the chocolate cherry slowly, mindfully, enjoying every bite. Before taking another bite, look at the candy. Breath the alluring scent of the chocolate and the sweetness of the cherry in and out, in and out. Imagine the sweetness of the small but powerful cherry cordial permeating your life, the life you are living to the fullest.

Manifest Now!

Once you promise yourself to live every day to the fullest, you'll discover a whole new way of living. You live with purpose and a keen understanding of what you seek. As you begin to implement your plan, your life changes and improves beyond what you expected.

Sit or stand in a comfortable position. Hug yourself the way you would want someone you love to hug you. Think of the sweetness of the chocolate-covered cherry cordial and feel the pleasure of eating it slowly, truly tasting each bite. You want to taste life's sweetness every day, to live your best life.

Repeat these words with passion and conviction: "I live my life to the fullest by making it a priority to show my love more deeply in my words and actions to those I care about most. I live my life to the fullest by moving one step closer to my goals each day. I am awake and aware of what my priorities are, and I strive to meet them by living each day to the fullest. All is well. It is done."

Affirmations for Living Each Day to the Fullest

- Each day I wake up with a plan to spend it wisely.
- I live with a purpose and a deep understanding of what I'm seeking.

- I tell those I cherish how much I love them in words and deeds.
- I draw up an action plan to realize my goals and dreams.
- I take small steps each day to reach my goals.
- Starting now, I am beginning to live each day to the fullest.
- Each day I move one step closer to my best possible life.

8

Live with a Light Heart

Consider This

Do you tend to take what others say too seriously? Are you so sensitive that the slightest negative remark from a family member or friend catapults you into anger or sadness? You wish you didn't take things so deeply to heart and that you could learn to laugh more and cry less. Maybe you've always been this way. You wonder if it's too late to change your reaction to people when they rattle you, to take it lightly instead of heavily, to let it simply fade away instead of giving it credence.

It all comes down to you and whether you choose to respond negatively or positively when people upset you with what they say or do. If you respond negatively, you're likely to hurt yourself and find heaviness rather than lightness in your life.

It doesn't help to let resentments build up and over-flow, causing you physical and psychological distress.

Consider telling people that what they've said bothers you. If this doesn't help, remember that some people don't think when they speak and that it doesn't pay to take them seriously.

Tread lightly along your path, and live with a light heart. Life is short. Do everything you can to enjoy it.

Meditation for Living with a Light Heart

When people criticize you or say negative things to you, you feel hurt and upset. You want to react differently so that what others say doesn't affect you so deeply. Whenever you find yourself taking things too seriously, say "Stop" in your mind. Resist the impulse to react. Sometimes the person criticizing you doesn't realize she's doing it. Other times the person knows he said something hurtful, but it's his nature to speak this way; therefore, it is his problem, not yours.

Take a moment to breathe in the color yellow, the shade of lightheartedness. Picture a vibrant yellow canary singing in a green, leafy tree. The canary is messaging you with its song: "Relax, stay calm, feel as light as I do singing this song for you now." Think of the yellow, and slowly breathe it in and out, in an out. Nothing can bother you. The yellow surrounds you like a shield and helps you live with a light heart.

Manifest Now!

Hold your palms up so that you can feel the lightness of the canary yellow color enter your hands and travel through your whole body. You are lighter than air, light as the spirit inside your body.

As you breathe the yellow in and out, say these words aloud: "I feel relaxed and lighthearted even when people say things that hurt or upset me. I listen to what they say, but I do not let it disturb or bother me, for it is their way of thinking, not mine. I am confident in myself and take what others say in a lighthearted way. It is always my choice whether to accept or reject other people's opinions about how I should live my life. I am lighthearted, positive, and calm."

Affirmations to Help You Live with a Light Heart

- I choose to respond to criticism in a lighthearted way.
- When someone says negative things, I stay calm and do not take it personally.
- I see critical people for who they are and know it is what I believe that counts.
- I choose to respond calmly rather than react when someone upsets me.
- When someone says things that bother me, I let it pass and don't dwell on it.
- I choose the way I respond to people. I am always in control of the way I respond.
- I am lighthearted and positive in all my interactions.

9

Give and Receive Love

Consider This

Do you ever find yourself blocked when it comes to giving and receiving love in a relationship? If you crave love in your life but aren't receiving it, think of what you can do to make it materialize for you. If you find your relationship rewarding, what can you do to enhance it? Ask yourself what you can do to attract and enjoy a harmonious, satisfying relationship.

Once you're in a relationship, how can you avoid patterns that tear at its fabric and cause needless drama? What can you and your partner do to ensure a smooth, peaceful path? Everyone experiences conflicts, but what can you do to ensure that romance and mutual respect flourish side by side? Think of ways you can build each other up even when you feel frustrated by each other's flaws and foibles.

Think about giving and receiving love. What can you do to attain the relationship you want and need? How much are you willing to compromise, to change what you believe a successful relationship should mean for both parties? After all, the only person you can truly change is you. If you look for your partner to change, it may never happen.

If you're not happy with your relationship the way it is and you feel it may not be what your heart desires, you may want to reconsider it within the context of what is right for you at this time in your life. You are a worthy person who deserves to give and receive love. If you look for love in a spirit of complete awareness, you will find it.

Your desire is to give and receive love that is exciting and blissful, yet calm and peaceful, without undue drama or game-playing: just love, pure and simple, as close to heaven as you can get on earth.

Meditation for Giving and Receiving Love

The universe is working in your favor to help you enjoy a constant, caring relationship that enhances your life. This love is the hub of the wheel around which everything else revolves. Cross your hands over your heart and feel your capacity to give and receive love, a pure and simple, yet sublime love that does not criticize or judge, the love you were born to enjoy.

Visualize the color pink you like best, your favorite shade of pink: the delicate pink of a tea rose or a bold pink sunset streaking a deep blue sky. Breathe your perfect pink in and out slowly. The pink infuses your body with a capacity for deep and enduring love. Breathe the pink you love best in and out, in and out. The love you need is part of your soul, your psyche. It is yours if you ask and believe. So be it.

Manifest Now!
Use one of the following two scripts:

If you are already in a relationship:
Open your arms wide to embrace the mutual love that comes your way, the love you give and receive. Thinking of the pink that helps you give and receive love, say these words aloud. As you say them, open your arms wide to embrace the mutual love that comes your way, the love you give and receive. "I am giving and receiving love to the fullest extent. My relationship is improving each day because I know that I can only change myself and not my partner. I know this love is right for me, and it is growing stronger each day."

If you are seeking a relationship:
Open your arms wide as you say these words to show your receptivity to the love that is coming your way: "I am finding a harmonious relationship with someone who loves me beyond compare and whom I love as a soul mate. It is done."

Affirmations to Help You Give and Receive Love

- I am giving and receiving love that brings me joy and completes my life.
- I am experiencing love that makes me feel uplifted and positive.
- I find new ways every day to nourish and enhance my relationship.
- I express my feelings honestly and ask the one I love to do the same with me.
- I build harmony and balance in my relationship by practicing empathy and understanding.
- My love and I complement each other and work together to make our relationship the best it can be.
- My love relationship grows more and more fulfilling each day.

10

Choose a Daily Spiritual Practice

Consider This

If you want to live your best life possible, choose a daily spiritual practice. This will help release any stress and tension you feel and will improve your mood and thinking skills. Once you launch your practice, it will also enhance your creativity. Best of all, you will feel more loving and kind toward everyone you meet throughout your day.

Meditation is not a religion or a belief system and can help you grow spiritually. Your daily practice can be simple and basic, like meditating using your breath as a mantra. As an alternative to using your breath, you may want to choose a word that is meaningful to you or even a pleasing sound that carries no meaning, to help you focus when thoughts intervene. Another form of meditation, such as the Kirtan Kriya, uses hand motions along with a mantra. If you get restless meditating, this may be a good type of practice for you. (Look at a u-tube video by Mia Haber that explains this practice. Here's the link: https://www.youtube.com/watch?v=1OWM2J4IgKg)

You have the freedom to choose the length of your practice. You can do it as little as five or six minutes once a day or for longer periods, such as twenty minutes, once or twice a day.

If you prefer another spiritual practice, such as prayer, feel free to go with whatever makes you feel comfortable. You can even combine prayer with meditation by saying a short one or two-word prayer as a mantra. Whatever you choose for your spiritual practice will give you a needed break from your daily activities and help improve your life in every way.

Meditation for Choosing a Daily Spiritual Practice

If you're not already involved with a spiritual practice, find one that appeals to you. Try it for a week or two. Then decide if it's the right one for you. If not, try another until you find the one that best suits your personality and lifestyle. If you're already involved in a practice, and you're happy with it, stay with it. If you'd like to experiment with a different practice, consider trying another to see which one you like best. The bottom line is to see which one can most effectively soothe your mind, body, and spirit.

Get comfortable, and in your mind, surround yourself with pure white, the cool color of snow. Feel the invigorating touch of the white snow on your face, arms, and legs. Breathe in the whiteness, and slowly exhale the dazzling brightness of slowly falling snow. Breathe the whiteness in and out, in and out, until you feel uplifted and energized as you do when you engage in your spiritual practice.

Manifest Now!

Imagine calmness and wisdom coming into your body, mind, and spirit as you inhale the pristine whiteness of gently falling snow. You are reveling in the timeless art of connecting with your higher self, where your intuition and perfect love for people and the universe finds its home. You and your spirit are one when you devote time to a spiritual practice.

Lift your hands to the sky, and say these words to strengthen your resolve to devote time to your practice: "I devote time to my spiritual practice every day to reap all the joy I can from my life. Everything seems to fall into place when I take the time to participate in my practice. I am more positive; I feel better physically and am more in touch with myself and others. I am grateful for the benefits my practice brings. Thank you."

Affirmations for Choosing a Spiritual Practice

- Adding a spiritual practice to my life makes my body, mind, and spirit thrive.
- A spiritual practice helps me feel more relaxed and lessens stress.
- I enhance my thinking skills when I engage in a spiritual practice.
- My creativity flourishes when I'm faithful to my practice.
- My spiritual practice increases my capacity for loving-kindness.
- I choose the spiritual practice that's perfect for me.
- My practice imparts calmness and wisdom to my body, mind, and spirit.

11

Find Joy in Little Things

Consider This

What things bring you the most joy in life? Some say it's having enough money to live comfortably, while others find happiness spending time with friends and loved ones or traveling to far-off lands. Everyone has different expectations for a happy life. Most people agree that it's the little things they experience daily that bring them the most joy, like spending time with children and seeing things through their eyes. Appreciating wonders of nature, such as basking in the sun, playing in the ocean, or skiing down a snowy slope, brings a sense of physical and emotional satisfaction often unparalleled by expensive material things.

Once you identify little things in your life that bring you a blissful feeling, think about finding more opportunities to enjoy them. Do you miss your friend from high school and haven't visited in a long time?

Call today and plan to get together. Are you so bogged down with work projects that you feel like flopping into your chair and watching TV when you get home? Spend time on your hobby instead: paint a picture, do a dance, write a story. You'll find a hidden reservoir of energy you never thought you had.

What about that book you've wanted to read or the movie you'd planned to see but couldn't find the time? Buy the book or find it in the library. Make time to see the movie on the big screen before it goes to video. There's no better time than now.

Make a list of little things that bring you joy and try to do one or more a week. Ask those you love what shared small experience would bring them joy, and engage in it together. Make memories that will stay in your heart more than anything money can buy.

Meditation for Finding Joy in Little Things

Transform your life by finding joy in little things each day. Take some time today to lose yourself in the moment. Freeze frame the experience and the joy you extract from it, and make it last. Observe how experiencing these little, yet transformative, moments can make an ordinary day memorable.

Relax your body and your mind. Bring the color cream into your mind. Picture the cream that adds richness to sweet berries: mellow, flavorful light cream. Slowly breathe in and slowly exhale the off-white creamy color, making yourself receptive to the small joys you are experiencing today. Breathe the light cream color in and out, in and out. Inhale its light but rich goodness as you take in the small joys that await you each day.

Manifest Now!

Focus on the happiness you get from observing small pleasures each day. Think of the richness of the color cream and how partaking of small joys will awaken your senses and enrich your spirit. Give gratitude for small joys like enjoying the company of friends and family, a delicious dinner, or a walk in the park where you can commune with nature.

Place your hands in a prayerful position and say these words: "I look forward to finding new ways to discover joy in little things. Every day new surprises await me and make me feel like I am unwrapping an unexpected gift from the universe. I open myself to the small pleasures granted me. I give thanks."

Affirmations for Finding Joy in Little Things

- Little things in life often bring me the most joy.
- I discover more opportunities each day to find joy in little things.
- I make finding joy in small things a priority.
- Every day, I think of little things that bring me pleasure and do them.
- I am mindful of the time I spend enjoying small pleasures.

- When I find joy in simple things, I make an ordinary day extraordinary.
- I am thankful for finding joy in little things each day.

12

Smile and Laugh More Often

Consider This

It's a fact that we tend to smile and laugh less as we become adults. That's understandable because responsibilities increase as we grow older and sometimes weigh us down. What would happen if you decided to smile and laugh more often? Smiling and laughing often can help you lead a magical life. For one thing, smiling and laughing releases endorphins that can lower your stress level and help lessen physical pain. Putting on a happy face also prompts others to find you more attractive, both physically and emotionally.

You may not feel like smiling or laughing, but when you make a conscious effort to do so, it has the same effect as if you had something to be happy about. Research shows that your brain can't tell the difference, and yet you reap all the benefits. If you smile and laugh more often rather than looking somber or disgruntled, it will become second nature to you to show positivity and cheerfulness. Better yet, smiling and laughing is contagious, prompting those around you to respond similarly.

Along the same lines, look for happy people to fill your friendship list, in both the real world and the virtual world of social media. Being around constant negativity puts a damper on your good mood. Think of how you feel coming away from a person who constantly complains or looks on the dark side of every situation. Conversely, consider how upbeat and optimistic you feel when you're in the company of someone who meets life with an uplifting attitude with smiles and laughter to match.

Meditation for Smiling and Laughing More Often

If you want to laugh and smile, give these two natural mood boosters a more prominent place in your daily life. If laughing and smiling challenges you, seek out positive, happy people to emulate. Watch funny movies, read humorous books, or scan the Sunday comics. Once you get into the habit of smiling and laughing, your life will turn a corner.

Buttercups impart lightness and joy. Imagine coming across buttercups growing wildly in your backyard. The delicate yellow buttercups brighten your mood and make you smile. Breathe in the summery yellow and bring happiness into your life's inner core. Breathe out any tension, tiredness, or pain you feel. Breathe the dazzling buttercup yellow in and out, in and out.

Manifest Now!

Make time to smile and laugh every day. Be mindful of the difference it makes in your attitude, your stress levels, and your overall feeling of good health. Think of the cheerful yellow buttercups brightening your day, the way you feel when you smile and laugh.

Standing, lifting your arms to the sky, say this: "I open myself to sunny moods by smiling and laughing more often. I surround myself with happy people who spread cheer and good-will because I know their moods can easily affect mine. When I smile and laugh, I tread more lightly, and the world looks better and brighter. I am happy and I show it. All is well."

Affirmations to Help You Smile and Laugh More Often

- Smiling and laughing more can bring a new dimension to my life.
- Showing cheerfulness improves my mental and physical health.
- Others see me more favorably when I smile and laugh more often.
- When I surround myself with positive people, I become more positive.

- Watching happy shows or reading humorous books makes me smile more.
- I make time to laugh and smile every day.
- My mood and attitude improve when I smile or laugh.

13

Enjoy Friendships

Consider This

Everyone is so busy these days that we often neglect friendship, one of the most important ingredients for a happy life. When you think about it, it takes very little effort to call, e-mail, or text a good friend and plan to meet. You don't have to make it an all-day get together if you're pressed for time. Meet for lunch or at home for a catch-up conversation. You'll be happy you made an effort.

Many benefits spring from seeing friends regularly. Sharing pleasant information about your life rekindles the joy you experienced during that time and helps you re-live it by bringing the memory to life. Additionally, sharing favorite activities with a friend can make them twice as pleasurable. Conversely, discussing problems or challenges with a friend helps you deal constructively with issues that concern you, often softening their effects on you.

Think of what you like doing most in your spare time. Do you like to explore museums, see movies, or go out to eat? Connect with a friend, and see how much more pleasure your favorite pastimes give you.

Meditation for Enjoying Friendships

You're feeling bogged down with worries about work, meeting your expenses, or coping with the daily grind. You want to find time for your friends and wonder if it's possible, given your busy schedule. All you have to do is make a call, send a text or e-mail, and arrange a friend date. Think about the joy you experience every time you meet with a friend.

When you think of rekindling your friendships, envision the color sky blue, the color that makes you happy and content, the way you feel with friends. Relax and slowly breathe in the color of a heavenly blue sky. Picture a clear blue sky, no clouds in sight. Breathe in and out the sight and scent of a balmy sky-blue night. Breathe the sky blue in and out, in and out.

Manifest Now!

No matter how busy your day, month, or year is, take time to reach out to a friend to help a friendship grow and flourish.

Standing, hold your arms at waist level and open them wide, palms up, to let the light of friendship into your life. Say these words aloud: "I open myself to the glorious gift of friendship. I stay connected to those with whom I share a special bond, the people I love to be with to think about the past, and look forward to the future, but most of all, to take pleasure in the present. I am making a conscious effort to reach out to friends I've known and loved over the years and to the new ones I've made. I am making the time to enrich my life with the gift of friendship. And so it is."

Affirmations for Helping You Enjoy Friendships

- I make time for friends so my life is complete.
- No matter how busy I am, I keep in touch with friends
- I listen with an open mind and heart when my friends confide in me.
- Friendships are one of life's greatest treasures. I make friendships a priority.
- I am never too busy to talk to a friend.
- No matter what happens, good friends will always listen as I will to them.
- I take the time to schedule an activity that my friend and I enjoy.

14

Be There for Others

Consider This

Being a friend is easy when everything's going well. However, the true measure of friendship reveals itself when one friend is willing to go out of the way for another. For example, your friend is having relationship or family problems. Your willingness to listen with kindness and empathy can deepen your bond of friendship.

It can be challenging to listen to a friend's problem with relationships, work, or other personal difficulties without interjecting your advice or solutions to remedy the problem. Often, listening without judging is all the person needs to realize a good resolution. If your friend is having a hard time making an important decision, putting yourself in his place without telling him what to do goes a long way toward helping him know he's loved and valued.

Besides listening with loving-kindness to a friend's concerns, friendships flourish when you take the time to check in on your friend about how she's feeling and what's new in her life. The gift of time spent with a friend means more than any expensive material gifts. However, small items such as books, music, or a favorite homemade food are good ways to show friends how important they are to you. Heartfelt handwritten notes on greeting cards for special occasions or for no particular reason can strengthen a friendship more than numerous texts or phone calls. They're tangible evidence that you'll always be there for your friend.

Meditation for Being There for Others

Being there for your friend in good times and bad helps your friendship flourish. You enjoy one another's company, and you also support one another when life throws you curve balls. You can provide anchors for one another by always being available to listen without imposing your ideas about how to proceed when a problem arises.

Get comfortable and think of a cluster of light green grapes, lightly sweet but tart to the taste and bursting with moist goodness. Mindfully breathe in and exhale out the pale green color of grapes. Imagine the taste of a sweet green grape, ingesting its healthful juice. Breathe the color of pale green grapes, in and out, in and out.

Manifest Now!

Get more out of your friendships by giving more. Think of the mellow green color of a cluster of sweet green grapes. Your friendships are mellow, like the taste of grapes, mellow, and lasting. Good friendships make life sweeter.

Rest your palms on your legs and say this aloud: "My friendships are a major part of what gives my life meaning. I listen mindfully to my friends and put myself in their place when they tell me their concerns or ask for advice. I show my friends I care about them by being there when they need me. I send blessings to my friends."

Affirmations for Being There for Others

- I listen to my friend with empathy and without judgment.
- I put myself in my friends' places to better understand their situations.
- I take the time to check in with my friend.
- I give my friend small, thoughtful gifts that show I care.
- Being there for my friends makes my friendships grow.
- I support my friends as I want them to support me.
- I gain more from my friendships when I give more.

15

Love Learning

Consider This

Learning is the key to staying vital in mind, body, and spirit. When you make an effort to learn something new, you feel energized and alive. Make it a point to map out what you'd like to learn and find the best place for you to learn it.

Think of how you learn best, and go that route to learn a new skill or to learn more about something you already know. Do you learn best by taking a course with lessons and assignments, or would online instruction that allows you to learn at your own pace and in your own time suit you better? Maybe you'd prefer to delve into a new interest by researching a topic in your own way, using a combination of books and online resources.

Learning something new that enlivens and awakens you gives you a new perspective on life. If you're in a rut, it takes you out of it and gives you a new way of looking at things. When life becomes humdrum, learning by building on what you already know or by learning something new helps you reinvent yourself.

Meditation for Loving Learning

What would you like to learn? This is the day you will begin to look into something you have always wanted to know, something that has always sparked your interest. Picture yourself doing one thing today to bring you closer to your goal of learning about something you love; then start to bring that knowledge into your life.

Think about the color gray when you think about learning something you love. Picture a vibrant, silvery gray swirling in your mind to activate your desire to fully understand a subject that will awe and inspire you to new heights. Relax and slowly breathe in the silvery gray of a downy quilt that calms and comforts you in the shivery coldness. Breathe the silvery gray in and out, in and out. You feel the gray infused with silver activating your mind to take the first step to learn something that interests you, something that nourishes your soul.

Manifest Now!

Make the decision today to learn about something that excites and empowers you. Feel the warmth and lightness of the silvery gray quilt.

Lift your palms to the air and say aloud: "I revitalize my life when I open myself up to learning. I begin my quest for knowledge with an open mind and heart. I explore all possibilities to help me achieve my goal. At this moment, I commit myself to learn about something that enlightens my life, something I have always dreamed of doing. No matter how busy I am, I permit myself to spend time learning about what I love."

Affirmations to Help You Love Learning

- I love learning new things and increase my knowledge each day.
- I am curious about learning new skills and find ways to incorporate them into my life.
- I build on skills I already possess and find new ones to embrace.
- I consider what helps me learn best and use this approach when learning about something I love.
- If I have questions about learning what I love, I find the answers easily.
- Learning about things that interest me brings meaning to my life.
- Discovering things to learn and love gives new purpose to my life.

16

Share Your Knowledge

Consider This

One of the greatest joys you can experience is sharing your knowledge with others. Teaching is second nature to all of us as we help people progress in positive ways throughout their lives. You can teach as a parent, coworker, or friend. You can try teaching someone a skill that's second nature to you, like cooking, painting, writing, or another language. Watch your student's eyes light up as he processes the new information you impart and learns how to master it. Then he, in turn, can share the knowledge with someone else in a chain that will influence many lives.

You can start by helping a friend or family member master a subject she's always wanted to learn. If you feel you have expertise in a certain area, you can also volunteer or get paid to give talks on the topic. Community organizations, such as scouting or senior centers, are always searching for speakers who bring enthusiasm to their subjects. Similarly, opportunities abound to assist teachers as volunteers in schools or senior communities. Teaching a new skill helps diminish older peoples' loneliness and helps give them a sense of purpose and something to look forward to, two important qualities often lacking in seniors' lives.

How can you share your knowledge with someone and benefit in the process? Each of us has something we excel in that can bring a feeling of enthusiasm and renewal to others. Learning about a new subject or acquiring a new skill is a gift that the recipients enjoy for the rest of their lives. It will also provide a source of satisfaction for you, the imparter of knowledge.

Meditation for Sharing Your Knowledge

Your life becomes more meaningful when you share your knowledge with others. When you have a hobby or interest you enjoy, you can give that same feeling of being immersed in something you love to someone else.

Think of deep yellow zinnias with a honeycomb shape lining a path to a rustic country cottage. The lush golden color of saffron brings to mind the changes that fall brings, like the beautiful changes you plant in another soul when you share your knowledge. Slowly breathe in the saffron color of zinnias lining a garden path until you feel their splendor. Breathe the golden yellow in and out, in and out.

Manifest Now!

Contemplate the feeling of satisfaction that sharing your knowledge generates in your mind and heart. See yourself helping someone learn a new skill or enjoy a hobby that can bring a positive dimension to her life.

Move into a cozy position and say these words with conviction: "I make time to be a teacher to someone who needs my help. I hold the lamp of knowledge and pass it on to another soul with reverence and love. This person will pass it on to another soul, and the chain will continue to blossom and grow like an elegant golden flower. I am happy to share my knowledge with others."

Affirmations to Help You Share Your Knowledge

- Sharing my knowledge with others satisfies me.
- I'm making it a point to teach someone a skill I enjoy.
- I'm finding a way to teach my skills by volunteering.
- The young and elderly are good audiences for sharing my knowledge.
- Sharing my knowledge teaches me as much as it does the recipient.
- Those I teach will always carry the knowledge with them.
- The people I teach will share what they learn in a chain that continues.

17

Appreciate Beauty

Consider This

If you pondered what makes your life miraculous, one thing that would stand out would be your ability to appreciate all the beautiful elements of it: the beauty of the people you love, the magical sights that surround you every day in nature, and the miracle of each new day unfolding.

Caught up in your daily routine, it's easy to overlook the beauty that surrounds you. If you are truly in the moment and acknowledge the beauty that marks your days, you'll enjoy a new dimension of life, one that brings you closer to your connection with spirit, which is what you truly are. Colors will shine more brightly, casual conversations with those you love will become more memorable, and you will gain a new appreciation for each day you live.

Take the time to stop and cherish the beautiful people and things in your life. Look and truly see, listen, and truly hear, touch, and truly feel. See how your life changes when you become mindful of the beauty in your life. The beauty that surrounds you will brighten your days and bring you to a whole new level of existence that will greatly enhance the quality of your life.

Meditation for Appreciating Beauty

Consider how much more meaningful your life will become if you take the time to appreciate the beauty of the people and things you encounter each day. Take a moment now to witness how beauty works in your life to bring you a sense of joy and contentment, such as a special moment spent with someone you love, the glorious unfolding of nature's wonders throughout the seasons, and the distinctive pleasures you experience in hearing music, viewing art, or pursuing your unique individual passions.

When you think of appreciating beauty, imagine the color rose pink. Relax and breathe in the rose-pink scent of roses in a magical garden. You have nothing to do but breathe in the heady scent of roses and focus on the deep, deep pink of the flowers. Breathe the rose-pink in and out, in and out, until you and the sight and scent of the rose-pink become one.

Manifest Now!

Even when your day is filled with work or other meaningful activity, take some time to appreciate the endless beauty that surrounds you.

Sit in a relaxed position and rest your hands on your legs, palms up. Speak these words aloud: "I am mindful of the beauty in my life each day and appreciate it. The people I love, good friends, and those who come my way by chance are all beautiful in their own way. All manifestations of nature enhance my life and make me see, hear, and feel that I am privileged to be a part of this world. The beauty of art, music, and the interests that I pursue bring beauty to my world. Thanks to the Divine Spirit."

Affirmations for Appreciating Beauty

- I am conscious of the beauty that surrounds me every day.
- I appreciate the beauty in my life and am thankful for it.
- Each day, I am open to seeing beauty manifest in my life.
- Those I love and those who love me radiate beauty.
- I am aware of the beauty of nature and take time to enjoy it.
- I look forward to seeing the beauty of each new day.
- Beauty surrounds and uplifts me every day of my life.

18

Be Open to New Ideas

Consider This

It's easy to get into a rut when you think about the same old things in the same way. Opening your mind to new ideas and ways of thinking can present a challenge because there's a certain comfort in holding on to ideas you grew up with that are now deeply ingrained in your life. However, once you begin to open your mind to new ideas, you begin to see the world differently. You start to question your previous ideas and are more likely to come to new conclusions about your own life and your place in the universe.

The first step in opening your mind to new ideas is to listen with a non-judgmental mind. Then, as you discuss new ideas with others who espouse them, you can decide for yourself if you want to embrace the ideas or retain your original views. You can also research these ideas on your own to ensure that you're getting information from reliable sources.

Being open to new ideas is a way to learn and grow. It will pave the way to new paths and ways of thinking that will benefit you in the long run. Even if you decide to keep the ideas you already have and not accept the new ideas, at least you will understand another point of view. That in itself signifies intellectual and emotional growth.

Starting today, expose yourself to different ideas by listening to different points of view. Talk to someone whose ideas differ from yours. Discuss, debate, and then draw your own conclusions. Watch news shows and read articles that espouse different viewpoints from yours. In the end, the choice is yours.

Meditation for Opening Yourself to New Ideas

If you're looking for a way to put a spark in your life, think about opening yourself up to new ideas. Read, think, discuss, and consider ideas you may not have given yourself the freedom to entertain in the past. What is it you want to know? Is what you've always believed the ultimate truth? Open your mind and your heart to learn new ways of thinking and believing. Even if you don't end up thinking differently, you will grow in empathy and understanding of another viewpoint.

To help you open yourself up to new ideas, visualize the color mint green. Taste the buttery coolness of a mint green candy. Savor the sweetness and bring to mind the mint shade. Do not fear considering new ideas. See if they are right for you. If so, accept them, and change your way of thinking. If not, you've broadened your thinking, and that can make you thrive and grow. Breathe the mint green in and out, in and out, until you feel the freshness of new ideas entering your life.

Manifest Now!

Bring a new perspective to your life by opening your mind to new ideas. Think about ideas in a different way than you usually do, and your mind will grow and expand beyond belief. It's your choice to retain what you've always believed or to change your mind.

Imagine the coolness and freshness of mint green. Raise your arms to waist level and say these words: "I open myself to new ideas. I listen to other points of view respectfully and objectively. I research these ideas and draw my own conclusions. I examine my ideas in light of new ones and decide whether to keep what I hold true or to change all or part of what I believe. My mind is open to new possibilities. I welcome new ideas."

Affirmations for Opening Yourself to New Ideas

- I am curious about learning new ideas.
- My mind is flexible and open to new ideas.
- I am willing to change if I find new ways of thinking that I like.
- I listen to others' opinions without judging or condemning their beliefs.
- I research ideas that I'd like to know more about.

- Intellectual growth through exploring new ideas is one of my main goals.
- Whether I accept new ideas or keep the old ones I have, I keep an open mind.

19

Awaken Your Intuition

Consider This

It helps in all areas of your life to awaken your intuition. How do you know when your intuition is trying to give you a message? These messages can come in the form of a strong impulse to act on a feeling or as a small whisper that you have to listen well to hear. No matter which way intuition beckons, it will prove highly effective in helping you address your life questions.

Sometimes you rack your brain thinking about how to solve a problem when all you need to do is ask your higher self, which always knows the best path to take. The solution often eludes you the more you access your logical mind. Once you relax and let an answer come to you intuitively, you can let your logic and reasoning kick in and help you know how to proceed.

To determine whether your intuition is working to give you the best solution to your problem, ask yourself how you feel in your gut when you think about trying one solution over another. Does it feel right to you, or do reservations creep in to make you wonder if you're moving in the right direction? Also, consider how you feel emotionally about what you think your intuition is telling you. Do you feel relaxed and peaceful when you think about following the intuited advice, or does thinking about it make you feel tense and uneasy? You can easily test whether you're accessing intuited information by tuning in to the way your mind and body react.

When trying to tap into your intuition to gain the best advice possible, make yourself calm by finding your favorite way to relax: meditate or engage in an activity you find restful, such as reading or taking a walk in nature. During these times, when your body and mind feel rested and peaceful, you'll be more likely to jumpstart your intuition. Once you feel secure in relying on your instincts to find answers to your questions, the more prominent a part intuition will begin to play in your life.

Meditation to Help Awaken Your Intuition

As you begin to use your instincts to help you address any dilemmas that come your way, you'll feel more confident in your ability to come up with the right answer to any problem you face. After an answer presents itself, test it against your physical and emotional reactions and clues to see if you feel comfortable with it. If you do, you're on your way to using your intuition to solve any problem your face.

Relax your body and your mind. Bring in the color violet, the shade of a simple yet sublime flower. Think about the purple-blue hue of violets growing freely in a meadow. Slowly breathe in and slowly exhale the purple-blue violet color until you feel its wisdom permeate your spirit and make your intuition thrive. Breathe the color violet in and out, in and out.

Manifest Now!

Think of the benefits of awakening your intuition. You'll find a reliable answer you can depend on instead of worrying about solving your problem. Simply relax your mind and body, and let the answer come naturally and effortlessly. Have faith that you'll find the best solution to your question, and it will happen.

Set your body and mind at rest, and put the tips of your fingers on your third eye, located on your forehead between your eyebrows. Say these words: "I awaken my intuition and call on it to steer me in the right direction with any questions I have. I trust my intuition fully and know that it will always come up with the best possible answer in any situation that life brings me. When I follow my intuition, I connect with my higher self, which always knows the best path possible for me. All praise and honor to the Divine."

Affirmations

- Awakening my intuition helps me in all areas of my life.
- Intuitive messages come in the form of a strong impulse to act or as a whisper.
- Each time I use my intuition, it becomes stronger and more reliable.
- My higher self always knows the best path to take.
- To determine if my intuition is working, I consider mind and body signals.
- To tap into my intuition, I put myself into a relaxed state.
- The more I use it, the more intuition becomes a prominent force in my life.

20

Access Your Common Sense

Consider This

Have you ever noticed that the more you think about things, the answer to your problem seems to elude you? When you intellectualize your problem and approach it with logic rather than common sense, you wonder if you'll find an answer that appeals to you. Instead of ruminating or depending totally on your logical mind, turn your problem over to that part of you that always knows the answer, your common sense.

The commonsense answer to problems often seems so simple that you dismiss it as something that can't help you. However, a simple answer is often the best and most practical approach to solving a problem, be it big or small. It doesn't help to think too deeply when searching for an answer. Turn the answer over to your intuition, and your common sense will guide you in the right direction.

Common sense doesn't require advanced degrees or impeccable credentials. It's something we all possess if we listen closely to our inner voice. You have only to ask yourself, "What would be the best approach to solving this problem that's bothering me?" When you're relaxed and free of worry, you can access your common sense more effortlessly. If you agonize over problems and wonder which path to take, try calling on your intuition and common sense.

Meditation for Accessing Common Sense

You want the answer to your problem to work, and you want it to be practical and easy to implement. Instead of depending totally on your logical mind and agonizing over a solution, turn your question over to your intuition, and then apply your common sense.

Fix your attention on the color dark brown to activate your common sense. Sit in a relaxed position, and breathe in the smell of brown leather. Feel the suppleness of the leather, and slowly breathe in its soft, pliant brownness. Breathe the brown in and out, in and out, thinking of how your common sense is moving you toward the perfect solution.

Manifest Now!

Although finding a solution to a problem seems hard, it's easy if you use both your intuition and your common sense.

Sit comfortably, thinking of the color brown, a comfortable, practical shade, and say these words: "I depend on my intuition and common sense to give me the best answer possible. I can find everything I need within myself. I let the answer come naturally without stress or strain. If the answer to my problem does not come to me immediately, I will wait with patience and hopeful anticipation. My intuition, boosted by my common sense, always leads me to the best path. So it is, and so it will always be."

Affirmations for Accessing Your Common Sense

- Using common sense, along with my intuition, leads me to the best answer.
- I am relaxed and at peace when I access my common sense.
- Common sense is constantly at my disposal.
- I use my intuition to find and then apply a commonsense solution to my problems.
- A commonsense answer comes to me promptly.
- Using common sense is the best way to help myself.
- I rely on my intuition and common sense to help me solve problems.

21

Learn and Grow Each Day

Consider This

As you know, learning continues long after school is out of session. Make it a point to learn something new about yourself, about others, about your world every day. When you learn, you continue to grow and evolve in spiritual and temporal knowledge. You move forward in your quest to shed your old skin and grow another, more enlightened, powerful one.

What do you want to learn today? When you wake up, imagine one way you'd like to learn and grow. Be mindful of moving toward that goal as you go about your day. For a certain amount of time, a week, a month, for instance, focus your thoughts on one area: mind, body, or spirit. Think of something that will help you develop in that area, and then after focusing on it for a while, evaluate your personal growth in that area. You may choose, instead, to pay attention to one area one day and then switch to another the following day. It's up to you, but whatever approach you take, be curious, and observe how you progressed because of what you've learned.

For example, you may want to concentrate on expanding your mind by studying a subject you previously avoided or lacked knowledge about. You may want to discover how to make your body function better or begin a program to help improve a physical problem. Similarly, if you want to learn more about the spiritual realm and how it can help you improve your life in every way, concentrate on learning one of the spiritual arts such as meditation, communing with angels, or manifesting your dreams.

As you make progress in your quest for knowledge, notice how your quality of life improves in the areas of self-discovery and physical and emotional health.

Meditation for Learning and Growing Each Day

You are discovering ways to learn and grow all the days of your life. You are launching an action plan to learn more about how your mind, body, and spirit work together to improve how you think and feel. Each day, you make progress and move ahead in your quest to live your best life.

Relax your muscles one by one, and settle into a position you find comfortable. Think about the color

China blue, the elegant color of plates, teapots, and vases, superimposed on a white background. See yourself in an antique shop, surrounded by artifacts in China blue. Which one will you choose? Which facet of your life will you focus on today: mind, body, or spirit? At your own pace, breathe in and exhale the classic shade of China blue until you feel alive and uplifted as you will when you learn and grow. Breathe the China blue in and out, in and out.

Manifest Now!

Think of how much you will learn and grow when you set your intention to progress in your knowledge of mind, body, and spirit. Every day you learn something that brings you closer to your quest to live your ideal life. You evolve mentally, physically, and spiritually to live happily and authentically on your terms, setting your own rules. Stretch your body so that you feel taller and stronger. Think of the color China blue and how it sparks your mind to do bigger and better things.

Say these words: "I am making a plan to learn and grow every day in all areas of my life. I feel more alive and energized because I devote myself to learning all I can about improving my life mentally, physically, and spiritually. I am evolving into the person I was meant to be. And so it is."

Affirmations to Help You Learn and Grow Each Day

- Every day I am learning something new about myself, about others, and my world.
- I continue growing and evolving in spiritual and earthly knowledge.
- I am thinking of new ways to learn and grow.
- As I learn and grow, I take stock of my personal growth in that area.
- I constantly work on developing my knowledge of body, mind, and spirit.
- As I learn and grow, I notice how my life improves in every way.
- I am evolving in all ways to live authentically on my terms.

22

Aim to Focus

Consider This

Sometimes with everything going on in your life, you find it hard to focus on what's happening in the moment, what you need to attend to now. Multitasking, electronic devices, and many distractions can take you away from goals you're trying to accomplish. Other diversions take you back into the past or catapult you into the future and worry about tomorrow.

How can focus on the present help you? For one thing, you can enjoy every moment more. Also, directing your attention to the task you're working on helps you get things done more efficiently because you're doing what you have to do instead of anticipating outcomes and wondering how everything will turn out.

What can you do to help you focus on what you want to do this moment? You can notice the sights, smells, and sounds that ground you in "the now." You can settle in and begin your task with complete attention and awareness of what you're doing while you're doing it.

When you aim to focus, you are attentive to your task, whether it's something as mundane as paying bills or something more challenging, like settling a dispute with a person or a company. Whatever it is, give each task your full attention, so you don't become mired in the discomfort of it and can attend to the task in the best way possible.

Meditation for Aiming to Focus

Focus on the moment, on "the now," what you need to do at this time, in this place. With no particular urgency, gently, slowly, be in "the now." What is it you want to accomplish, what do you want to do? Give it your full attention. You are achieving it as you want it to be.

Call the color orange into your mind, the dark orange of a dreamy harvest moon, large and looming in the autumn sky. Breathe in and out until the mystical orange becomes a part of your thinking, a part of your mind. The forcefulness of the dark orange urges you to aim to focus on whatever it is you want to do in the moment. See the harvest moon light up the autumn sky. Picture the moon, and see yourself focusing as you breathe the orange in and out, in and out.

Manifest Now!

Take the time to be mindful, to live in the moment, especially when you aim to focus on something you want to accomplish. Tune out what's keeping you from fully tuning in. Give the task you're doing your full attention.

Get into a comfortable pose and say these words aloud with full conviction: "I am alive and in the moment. I aim to focus on something I want to accomplish, big and small things alike. When I focus on the task I'm doing, I gain good results because I am fully focused and in the moment. I am fully alive to all my dreams and give my attention to what I want to do right now. So be it."

Affirmations for Aiming to Focus

- I put myself in the moment before I begin to focus.
- I focus fully on what I want to achieve.
- Big and small things come to me with ease when I aim to focus.
- Focusing on the task at hand helps me complete a job easily.
- Whether I find a task pleasant or unpleasant, focusing helps me carry it out.
- Aiming to focus helps manifest what I want to accomplish.
- I am fully living in "the now" and accomplishing all that I desire.

23

Challenge Yourself

Consider This

How do you challenge yourself to live more fully and authentically? When you challenge yourself, you raise your comfort zone's bar to reach for goals you seek to attain. Some challenges you think about working on may be job-related. Here's an example: Should you stay in a position that proves profitable but not enjoyable, or should you launch an entirely new career?

Another challenge you could face may relate to relationships, like finding someone to love or deciding whether to stay in or leave a relationship. Yet another challenge may involve finding success in an artistic pursuit, such as music, art, or writing. It's a challenge because these creative outlets are often highly competitive and sometimes fraught with disappointment and the pain of rejection.

When a challenge presents itself, the most important thing is to forge ahead with faith and optimism, believing you can succeed in meeting the challenge. Once you're satisfied that you've thoroughly researched ways of overcoming the obstacles in your path, start putting the mechanisms in motion to face your challenge and come out on top.

Although it's important to meet your challenge and you've done your best to overcome many obstacles, if you don't meet your original goal, don't give up. Think of what would make you happy even though you may have to reframe your original goal or look for other ways to find satisfaction in what you're seeking.

Challenging yourself is one of the most important ways you can progress in your life, mentally, physically, and spiritually. What is your major challenge, and how will you meet it?

Meditation for Challenging Yourself

Ask yourself what kind of challenge would change your life to bring you closer to your ideal existence. To find your answer, think of an area of your life that needs improvement, one that you'd like to work on to bring you closer to your definition of an ideal life. Soul-search until you identify this challenge, and take all steps necessary to meet it.

Think about a dazzling color, crimson red, bright red with a tinge of blue. Picture a crimson double peony, a warm flower with layers of soft petals emanating from the crown. You pick the crimson peony from your garden and inhale its soft, sweet fragrance. Breathe the fragrant crimson scent in and out, in and out, until you feel its strength suffuse your spirit.

Manifest Now!

Think of the crimson red color of a majestic peony. Surround yourself with its powerful fragrance that will boost your power to help you meet your challenge. Set your intention to meet your challenge head-on and work toward meeting it. You become closer to it each time you take another step in its direction. You are meeting your challenge now.

Rest your hands, palms down on your knees, and say this: "I challenge myself to work toward (state your intention). Each day I progress further toward my goal. I overcome any obstacles in my path and move onward until I attain what I need to live the life I want and deserve. I am hopeful. Thank you."

Affirmations

- I challenge myself to live more fully and authentically.
- I raise my comfort zone's bar to reach my goals.
- I forge ahead to meet my challenge with faith and optimism.
- I am meeting my challenge successfully.
- I never give up trying to meet my challenge.
- Challenging myself helps me progress mentally, physically, and spiritually.
- Meeting my challenge brings me one step closer to my ideal life.

24

Set and Meet Goals

Consider This

Goals keep you going. Without goals, your life can seem empty and aimless. It's important to aspire to something that makes you reach higher than you thought you could. Goals give you this opportunity. Sometimes you let yourself get in the way of setting and meeting goals because you don't believe you can realize them due to lack of time, energy, or confidence.

To reach your goals, you have to believe they are possible and within your reach. You have to believe you have or will find the resources needed to meet them. If you're willing to forge ahead to reach your goals and realize your dreams, surround yourself with supportive, loving people who will cheer you on along the way. Above all, believe your goals are within your reach and that with a strong intention, you will find the resources to realize them.

What is it that you want to accomplish today? Set your goals now, and let the excitement begin.

Meditation for Setting and Meeting Goals

Setting and meeting goals are easier than you think. List one or more goals that you consider important, and think about what you need to do to achieve them. Then think of the best way to go about implementing your ideas. Make the process easy and effortless, and you will find yourself setting and meeting goals with more exuberance and greater success.

As you meditate on setting and meeting goals, fix your attention on the color reddish-orange, the color of a burning bonfire, a bonfire you'll ignite to set a fire in yourself to reach your goals, no matter how challenging they seem. Close your eyes and listen to the crackling, snapping sound of the reddish-orange bonfire. Breath in the color of orange tinged with red. Breath the orange-red in and out, in and out, while you see yourself setting and meeting goals.

Manifest Now!

If you spend time beforehand setting goals, you'll find it easier to reach them. It will be a pleasurable process if you map out your plan ahead of time and then go with the intention to implement it once you clarify how you plan to do it. Hear the crackling sounds and see the vibrant colors of the red-orange fire awakening you to meet your goals.

Sit comfortably and open your palms on your lap. Say these words, believing you will plan and implement your goals to make them a reality: "I am an expert at setting the goals that will bring me a better life. I take the time to plan and think about exactly what makes me happy, what gives meaning to my life. It is done."

Affirmations to Help You Set and Meet Goals

- Setting goals prepares me for success in doing what I want.
- I list my goals and concentrate on achieving them, one at a time.
- I set goals easily and effortlessly.
- Goal-setting helps me get to where I want to go.
- I seek out people who will encourage and support my goals.
- I use positive, encouraging self-talk when setting my goals.
- I am focused and determined to meet my goals.

25

See a Task to Completion

Consider This

Once you embark on a task, you look forward to completing it. But if you think about the culmination, the result, the joys of throwing yourself into the task can easily elude you. Instead, try to find joy in each part of the job you're doing as you're doing it. Don't concern yourself only with the excitement you'll feel when it's completed. In fact, you'll be more likely to complete your task if you take it one step at a time.

So many of us enjoy the thrill of starting a new task, of challenging ourselves to grasp beyond our reach. Sometimes you achieve what you set out to do, but other times distractions get in the way and deter you from completing what you want to accomplish. In other words, it's easy to start something new, but not always easy to complete what you want.

If you want to complete a task, whether it's something mundane like de-cluttering your living space, or something more complex, like completing a painting or a novel, say your intention aloud and work on your task every day with your final goal in mind. Put everything you have into completing your task.

If you don't succeed in seeing your goal to culmination (realizing an uncluttered living space, or selling a painting or novel, for example), adjust your goal to make it more realistic, and try again. Eventually, you'll reach your goal or find one you like even better.

Meditation for Seeing a Task to Completion

In your quest to complete a task or accomplish a goal, you can't help but think about the result. Sometimes it overshadows the joy you find in immersing yourself in an activity that satisfies your soul. You yearn to see the results of all your efforts so much that you may lose sight of the joy you find in doing the tasks that lead up to it. Work toward completing your task, and experience happiness along the way.

When you envision seeing a task to completion, think of the color melon green. Picture a ripe honeydew melon in peak season. Envision the lovely light green color. Cut into its softness and savor its sweetness. Relax and slowly breathe in and out, in and out, the pale green, the spring green of a honeydew melon, luxurious in its ripeness.

Manifest Now!

You have the drive and ability to see any task to completion. All it takes is a strong intention and a desire to see your task accomplished.

Stand, and with strong intent, say these words aloud: "I see my task to completion with ease and efficiency. I enjoy each moment that leads me to my desired result. I delight in the process of working on my task, rather than fixing my attention on seeing the result. I am working on completing my task with love and joy. It is done."

Affirmations for Seeing a Task to Completion

- I set my intention before starting my task.
- I enjoy performing each step of my task as I am doing it.
- Whether my task is small or large, I devote the same effort to it.
- I take pride in my progress along the way.
- Using positive self-talk, I encourage myself to continue my task every day.
- My task is meaningful and keeps me interested and involved.
- I have the drive and ability to see my task to completion.

26

Welcome New Experiences

Consider This

Sometimes new experiences come into your life because you seek them out. You have a desire to travel, so you plan a trip. You want to earn a degree, so you enroll in school. However, new experiences sometimes enter your life serendipitously.

An old or new friend shows up at your doorstep or on social media, and you laugh and learn from one another. Will it work to both your advantages? You have to wait and see. A job opportunity opens up unexpectedly. Should you take it or stay in your old position? You have the chance to move to another location that is far from your present one. Consider how life would change for you. Would it be better or worse than where you're now living? In all these cases, the decision about whether you take the chance is totally up to you. Whenever new experiences come your way, you have to consider whether it's best to embrace or reject them, choosing the path that's right for you at the time.

Look at the opportunity with an open mind. Ultimately, even if you decide to decline to accept the chance to do something different, at least you've given it thoughtful consideration. In some cases, it may be better to stay in your old job if the reasons merit it, but in others, it's to your advantage to take a chance and try one that has always intrigued you. Maybe it would make all the difference in your life. Even if you decide not to try it, at least you've given the idea some thought.

Maybe a move seems like a monumental task, but possibly you've been entertaining the idea for a long time. Try writing down the pros and cons of moving at this time. Consider it from all angles. Then make your decision after you've explored all your options.

The bottom line is that it often enriches your life to welcome new experiences, whether you seek them yourself or they come to you unexpectedly. You never know how your life will change, and possibly improve if you take that leap of faith and keep your mind open to new ways of thinking and living.

Meditation for Welcoming New Experiences
Picture yourself amid a new experience you've anticipated for some time. Think of the joy and satisfaction

you'd gain by welcoming that experience and knowing that it will change your life in a positive way. Now imagine a new experience coming your way, a chance to do something you didn't think about doing on your own. Entertain all the possibilities in your mind. Think about whether the time and circumstances are right for you at this time. Whatever you decide will be the best decision as you know yourself better than anyone does.

When you think of welcoming new experiences, envision the color bright red. Hold out your hand and picture a red ladybug crawling up your arm, slowly, deliberately, bringing you a change that will rejuvenate you. Relax and breathe the bright red along with the lucky thoughts the ladybug offers you. Breathe the red in and out, in and out, whether or not you decide to welcome the new experience. It's all in your hands.

Manifest Now!

When you see an opportunity to welcome a new experience, consider how it would change your life for the better. Whether you initiate the change or it comes to you by chance, welcome it if you feel it's right for you. Visualize the bright red ladybug bringing you the courage to try something new.

Open your palms to give yourself a feeling of strength and flexibility. Say this: "I open myself to new experiences. If the experience is right for me, I welcome it and see it as an adventure and a gateway to a new and more fulfilling life. I am grateful to the Infinite Spirit."

Affirmations to Help You Welcome New Experiences

- I look forward to new experiences and welcome them.
- I am open to new experiences that come my way.
- I seek out new experiences and look forward to trying them.
- I love the sense of adventure that trying new experiences gives me.
- New experiences enlighten and enrich my life.
- I look at new experiences in a hopeful and positive way.
- I keep an open mind about welcoming new experiences into my life.

27

Learn from Past Experiences

Consider This

Although it's important to live in the present, it's also helpful to learn from our past experiences. Sometimes we repeat the same mistakes, often to our disappointment and detriment. However, if we become more mindful and conscious of our actions and their repercussions, we'll be less likely to get bogged down in the same patterns that caused problems for us in the past. If you find yourself having problems in one area of your life, look for similarities in patterns from your past. You can break yourself of unproductive and negative experiences in romantic relationships, employment, and interactions with the people around you if you think about what happened in the past and learn from it.

Imagine you've had a series of problematic love relationships. Ask yourself what the similarities are and make a decision to avoid the same pitfalls that drew you into relationships comparable to this one. If you see the relationship veering in the direction of others that brought you unhappiness, extricate yourself from the union before it becomes harder to break it off.

If you have recurring problems in your job, be curious and ask yourself if these problems seem like those you've experienced with other jobs or employers. If so, try to get to the root of the problem so you can begin to solve it. Learn from the past to see what the causes of your dissatisfaction are so that you can begin to address them constructively.

If you experience problems with relationships, see what worked in the past to remedy them. Most of the time, do you believe it's something that you or the other party precipitated, or was it a combination? Ask yourself what worked in the past to help you avoid conflicts and keep that in mind when navigating your current relationships.

Past experiences will often provide you with clues about enjoying a more satisfying life now and in the future. Look to the past while living in the present.

Meditation for Learning from Past Experiences

You are rooted in the present but look to the past for clues that give you an idea about improving your life. If you've made mistakes in the past, use them to work to your advantage by revisiting them but not dwelling on them. In this way, you'll gain insights to help you choose the direction that's right for you in relationships, jobs, and other crucial areas of your life.

Settle into a relaxed position and call upon the color of a juicy ripe pear, yellow-green with a touch of blush pink. Taste the slightly grainy sweetness when you eat the pear. It takes you back to your youth when you enjoyed the flavorful fruit. The past was good then, and it is good now as you begin to learn and grow from your past experiences. They can help guide you to a better life in the present. Slowly breathe the scent of the juicy pear in and out, in and out.

Manifest Now!

You look at the past, not to regress and ruminate over it, but to progress and move forward from what you learn. Experience no regret about what happened, but hold in your heart a strong resolution to learn all you can so you can enjoy your life now and in the coming years.

Stand, stretch your arms and legs and look up to the sky. Lift your arms to your waist, and hold your hands palms-up. Picture the yellow-green pear color with a tinge of pink, a cheerful color that brings back the past. Say this: "I use my experiences from the past as a guide to how I live in the present and the future. Everything I learned in the past teaches me something about this moment and the moments to come. I think about what happened in the past as a learning experience and a guidepost about how to live my best life now. All is well."

Affirmations for Learning from Past Experiences

- I live in the present, and I learn from my past experiences.
- When I have problems in an area of my life, I look to the past for insights.
- I look to the past to see the causes of my present problems to address them constructively.
- Past experiences give me clues about enjoying a more satisfying present and future life.
- I look to the past for insights while living in the present.
- The past provides the key to living my best life now.
- I progress in the present because of what I learn from the past.

28

Look Forward to Something

Consider This

Looking forward to something is one of the main things in life that keeps you going. Anticipating little things each day that bring you joy can make you feel positive and uplifted even in the face of temporary setbacks. Reading a favorite book, luxuriating in a tub, or enjoying a leisurely dinner with someone whose company you relish puts a spark in your day. Don't let a day pass without looking forward to something you consider satisfying and uplifting.

Thinking about something you're going to do in the future, like taking a trip or attending a special occasion, such as a reunion or a wedding, brings you a sense of heightened anticipation as you begin to prepare for the event. Isn't it true that the fun of planning for such an event equals or surpasses the excitement you feel when you go on the trip or attend the wedding?

When you were younger, you hadn't experienced as much, so often it seemed impossible to wait for the upcoming event, even if it was only a day away. As you grew older, you did similar things so many times that you may not derive as much excitement anticipating doing something you've waited for. Try shifting the way you look at things. Approach each event you look forward to as a child would, as if you're doing it for the first time. To truly enjoy each day, look at it as a new experience that you've never lived through before and may never see again.

Think about what you can look forward to today, and in the future, that will make your life more meaningful and exciting.

Meditation for Looking Forward to Something

Looking forward to something makes you feel alive and energized. Think of something you can look forward to, and make it a point to plan something to look forward to in the future. If you want to feel fulfilled and truly enjoy your life, don't let a day go by without having something to look forward to because the anticipation of doing something you find pleasurable can equal or surpass the experience.

Think about a sparkling emerald green stone set in a silver ring. Slip it on your finger and fixate on the vibrancy and hope the green signifies. The shimmering green revitalizes your spirit and gives you a hopeful sense of anticipation about looking forward to something. Looking forward to something always brings you hope that your life will be the best it can be today and in the future. Relax and slowly breathe the gleaming emerald green in and out, in and out.

Manifest Now!

Make looking forward to something for the short and long term, a goal you carry with you each day. Let your spirit take on the shimmering green of an emerald so that what you look forward to manifests and materializes to your liking.

Put your mind and body at ease, and lift your hands in a prayerful position. Say this: "Looking forward to something gives my life meaning and purpose. As much joy lies in anticipation of what I look forward to as in the unfolding of the event. I wake up with a sense of excitement and expectation that what I look forward to will renew my mind, body, and spirit. May it always be so."

Affirmations for Looking Forward to Something

- I feel alive and energized when I look forward to something.
- I look forward to something every day.
- I look forward to things with great enthusiasm as I did when I was younger.

- Looking forward to things now and in the future brings new excitement to my life.
- The fun of anticipating something is often as satisfying as experiencing it.
- Looking forward to something makes me feel alive and energized.
- When I look forward to something, it gives my life meaning and purpose.

29

Accept Yourself

Consider This

Accepting yourself can be easy when everything's going right in your life. However, when you encounter problems and pitfalls, sometimes you blame yourself for the way events turn out even when you weren't at fault. I'm sure you know that sometimes things happen for no reason at all and that you have little or no control over the outcome. Often, you're hard on yourself and think about what you could have done to realize a better resolution of your problem.

When you accept every part of yourself, your positive points and challenges, you proclaim your love for yourself and allow yourself to be human and make mistakes. Be gentle on yourself. Instead of directing your attention to your faults, think about your good points. When thinking about your friends, you're likely to see the best in them, emphasizing their positive qualities rather than stressing the personality traits that could annoy you if you let them. It's not that you don't think your friends have any negative traits, but that you accept them and don't let them overshadow the reasons you think highly of those you care about.

When you're tolerant of another person's imperfections, you see the good in them because it overshadows and outshines any flaws they have. Similarly, if you mainly see the good in yourself, it puts any faults you may have in perspective. Accepting yourself as you are makes you less apt to judge yourself and think less of yourself because of a few insignificant imperfections that others probably don't notice.

Accept yourself for how you act, how you deal with your life. Accept everything about yourself, including your physical appearance and emotional health. If you want to change anything about your mind, body, or spirit, you're free to do so, but be sure it's your decision and no one else's. Above all, accept and love yourself as you love others.

Meditation for Accepting Yourself

Think about how your life would improve if you showed yourself total acceptance. Showing yourself tolerance instead of expecting perfection, will help you gain a better appreciation of your positive attributes. It will also make you appear more confident in the outside world. You'll work better, get along with co-workers better, and enjoy your own company better than you have in the past.

Picture the austerity of maroon, a dark red, the plain and simple hue of a Buddhist monk's robes. Maroon represents your true self, exactly as you are, both good points and shortcomings. Mellow out until you feel the plush monk's robes surround you with total love and acceptance of yourself. Bring calmness to your mind and spirit. Breathe the maroon, the comforting dark red, in and out, in and out.

Manifest Now!

Set the intention to accept yourself now for exactly who you are. If you think you can improve yourself in some ways, work on it without putting yourself down or judging yourself. Speak of yourself in positive terms, and show yourself the compassion you show others in accepting them for who they are. As you begin to accept yourself, you will grow in empathy and kindness toward yourself and others. Commit today to accept yourself.

Feel the comfort of the maroon robe wrapped around your body, reaching into your mind and spirit. Cross your arms over your body and rub them gently in a warm, comforting motion. Repeat these words: "I accept and respect myself for who I am. The good things I do and say define me as a person. I am a worthy person who progresses along my path, always looking for the good within myself and others. I am grateful for who I am."

Affirmations

- I accept every part of myself, both my positive points and shortcomings.
- I am gentle on myself and think about my good attributes.
- I put any faults I have in perspective and don't judge myself.
- I accept everything about myself, including my appearance and mental health.
- If I want to change anything about myself, it is my decision alone.
- I accept and love myself as I accept and love others.
- I accept myself exactly as I am.

30

Love Yourself

Consider This

Loving yourself is simply accepting yourself for who you are. It's embracing yourself for your good points and weak points. It never involves judging or putting yourself down, and it doesn't call for comparing yourself to other people. You are perfect just as you are. You have unique talents and abilities that no one else has, and you are one of a kind, never to be repeated.

When you're tempted to be hard on yourself or to hold yourself to impossible standards that you wouldn't set for others, sit back, and appreciate yourself for who you are. Don't struggle to reinvent a better you because you are enough just as you are. That's not to say, don't work to better yourself or strive to realize your dreams. If you accept yourself and treat yourself with kindness and compassion as you would treat a dear friend, you will become more patient with yourself when you face stumbling blocks or rejection. Since you are fine just as you are, you will strive to reach your goals less effortlessly and without all the stress that often accompanies it.

Loving yourself means showing more patience with yourself when things don't go your way and not giving up easily when you face hardships or setbacks. If you love someone, your understanding knows no bounds, and you let them learn and grow at their own pace. Give yourself the same consideration you'd give others.

Self-love makes you more open to accepting others despite their faults and imperfections. It makes you a better listener, more open to granting empathy when someone needs to be heard and validated. When you love yourself unconditionally, you make room in your heart to love and care about others.

Are you ready to love yourself and accept yourself for who you are every day? Start with small steps. Think of one positive thing you've done each day and commend yourself for it. You are a worthy, perfect person.

Meditation for Loving Yourself

Think of the many positive attributes you have. Recall some of the things your family and friends praise you for and let those qualities guide you. What do you find most endearing about yourself: your capacity for love, your concern for others, or something else unique and individual to you alone? Picture yourself completely at peace with who you are and comfortable in your skin. You love yourself and treat yourself with kindness.

Imagine in your mind's eye a magenta balloon on a long string. The pink-rose color mesmerizes you and reminds you of a deep, abiding love, the love you have for yourself. Hold the balloon and inhale the majestic magenta hue. Inhale and exhale, inhale and exhale magenta, and feel the love you have for yourself. Then mentally release the balloon into the sky so it fills the air with love for yourself and others.

Manifest Now!

Accept yourself for who you are and love yourself by being gentle with yourself. You are whole and perfect as you are. Hug yourself like you're hugging your best friend. (That's you, by the way.) Picture the pink-rose hue of magenta washing over your heart, the center of love for yourself and others.

Say these words while embracing yourself: "I love myself and celebrate who I am. I love myself just as I am and focus on my good qualities. I am a unique person in the universe. And so it is."

Affirmations to Encourage Loving Yourself

- I love and accept myself for who I am.
- I am one of a kind, never to be repeated.
- I see myself as my best friend and helpmate.
- I celebrate my uniqueness as a human being.
- I appreciate and nourish my positive qualities.
- I build myself up with encouragement and praise.
- I treat myself with patience and kindness as I would a friend.

About the Author

Catherine DePino has written over 20 books for traditional publishers dealing with spirituality, Mindfulness, bullying, grammar/writing, and women's issues. Her bully prevention book, *Blue Cheese Breath and Stinky Feet: How to Deal with Bullies* (APA) is widely used in bully prevention programs and is published in different languages. Additionally, her articles have appeared in national magazines, such as *The Writer* and *The Christian Science Monitor*.

The author's educational background includes a bachelor's in English education, a master's in English and Spanish education, and a doctorate in curriculum theory and development and educational administration, all from Temple University. She worked for 31 years as a teacher and department head of English, world languages, social studies, and English as a Second Language in a large urban school district. After this, Temple University employed her as an assistant professor of education and a student teaching supervisor.

The author has a strong platform for the series, *Help Yourself : Magical Meditations to Soothe the Mind, Body, and Spirit.* In addition to her careers as an educator and writer, she engages in many spiritual practices. She has meditated using both the Transcendental (TM) approach, Mindfulness, and the Kirtan Kryia. Additionally, she studied the Tarot and psychometry for many years. Catherine is also a Reiki Master who offers hands-on healing for physical and emotional problems. The author also completed an in-depth course in Mindfulness meditation offered by Jefferson University. Mindfulness principles provide a philosophical base for the author's book in that she believes that "living in the now" will help readers realize a more fulfilling live in every way.

For many years, Catherine served on the board of directors of The Philadelphia Writers' Conference, where she worked on the speaker's bureau and community outreach committees. She is looking forward to discussing her forthcoming book with spiritual seekers across the country. Readers can access the author's website at http://www.catherinedepino.com

www.ingramcontent.com/pod-product-compliance
Lightning Source LLC
Chambersburg PA
CBHW031557040426
42452CB00006B/330

* 9 7 8 1 6 2 0 0 6 2 6 4 7 *